DEC 1 9 2008

D0953411

NELSON MANDELA

Essential Lives

NELSON
MANDELA
A LEADER FOR FREEDOM

by **Kekla Magoon**

Content Consultant:
Paul J. Kaiser, African Studies Center
University of Pennsylvania

ABDO
Publishing Company

CREDITS

Published by ABDO Publishing Company, 8000 West 78th Street, Edina, Minnesota 55439. Copyright © 2008 by Abdo Consulting Group, Inc. International copyrights reserved in all countries. No part of this book may be reproduced in any form without written permission from the publisher. The Essential Library™ is a trademark and logo of ABDO Publishing Company.

Printed in the United States.

Editor: Rebecca Rowell
Copy Editor: Paula Lewis
Interior Design and Production: Emily Love
Cover Design: Emily Love

Library of Congress Cataloging-in-Publication Data
Magoon, Kekla.
   Nelson Mandela / Kekla Magoon.
      p. cm. — (Essential lives)
   Includes bibliographical references.
   ISBN 978-1-60453-038-4
   1. Mandela, Nelson, 1918—Juvenile literature. 2. Presidents—South Africa—Biography—Juvenile literature. 3. Anti-apartheid activists—South Africa—Biography—Juvenile literature. 4. Apartheid—South Africa—History—20th century—Juvenile literature. 5. South Africa—Politics and government—1948–1994—Juvenile literature. 6. South Africa—Politics and government—1994—Juvenile literature. 7. South Africa—Race relations—History—20th century—Juvenile literature. I. Title.

   DT1974.M25 2008
   968.06'5092—dc22
   [B]
                        2007030842

TABLE OF CONTENTS

Nelson Mandela's clenched fist, a symbol of black power

TURNING POINT

*I*n late 1963, a trial began in South Africa that would become the most important trial in the nation's history. In the Rivonia Trial, Nelson Mandela and ten of his colleagues and friends stood accused of major crimes against their government. They were accused of planting bombs, planning a war, and building a secret army. Mandela entered the courtroom to the sound of a cheering crowd. The people shouted a call and response in support of Mandela and the freedom movement. "*Amandla*! (Power!)" some people called. "*Ngawethu*! (The power is ours!)" others replied.[1]

Mandela smiled when he heard the cheers. He raised his fist high in the air, and the people cheered even louder. He looked at the crowd that had gathered in the courtroom. He saw many familiar faces: his wife, his mother, his friends, and his partners. He also saw many strangers who had come to support him. Seeing all the people who believed in him gave Mandela strength. Mandela held his head high as he walked to his seat in the "dock," the area designated for the defense lawyers and the accused men.

The very serious charges against the accused included sabotage and conspiracy to overthrow the government. If the men were found guilty, they could face the death penalty. Mandela, a black South African lawyer, wanted to change

Mandela's Plea

When Justice de Wet asked Mandela at the beginning of the Rivonia Trial how he would plead, Mandela replied, "My Lord, it is not I, but the government that should be in the dock. I plead not guilty."[2]

the government. He had hoped to do so without bloodshed. Mandela had committed many of the acts he was accused of, but his actions had a greater purpose.

APARTHEID

At the time, South Africa was governed under a system known as *apartheid*, an Afrikaans word that means "separateness." Apartheid gave all political, social, and legal power to white South Africans, making them dominant to the nonwhite people living in South Africa, which included Indians,

---

Apartheid

Once the National Party controlled the South African government, many apartheid laws were created to systematically separate the races. The Prohibition of Mixed Marriages Act (1949) and the Immorality Act (1949) were the first apartheid laws. They made marriage and romantic relationships between the races illegal. The Population Registration Act (1950) assigned everyone in South Africa to a race. After the law was created, every citizen was given documentation that showed their assigned race.

Additional laws quickly followed that separated the races:

- The Group Areas Act (1950) defined areas by race, giving different areas of the country to different races.
- The Separate Representation of Voters Act (1951) made nonwhites less powerful in politics. Under this law, nonwhites were still allowed to vote. However, the politicians they elected had little or no power in government.
- The Bantu Authorities Act (1951) removed Africans' South African citizenship and the accompanying rights.

These and subsequent laws placed nonwhites at a disadvantage to whites in all areas of life.

coloureds (mixed race), and blacks. As a result, black South Africans were left with little power, even though they made up the majority of the population. They could not vote, hold political offices, work certain jobs, or live in the same neighborhoods with white people.

Mandela was a leader among a large group of black South Africans fighting to end apartheid. His freedom movement sought to create an equal society for black people and white people, as well as Indians and coloureds. Under apartheid, black South Africans had no legal power. The only way to fight for change was to step outside the law, which was not considered legitimate by a majority of white South Africans. Mandela and his friends knew that the white South African government would look upon their actions as criminal, but the men were willing to face the consequences because they believed deeply in their

Rivonia Trial Defendants

The men accused in the Rivonia Trial along with Nelson Mandela were:

- Walter Sisulu, a close friend and colleague
- Govan Mbeki, a close friend who lived in Rivonia
- Ahmed Kathrada (Kathy), an Indian activist
- Andrew Mlangeni, an activist
- Elias Motsoaledi, an activist
- Bob Hepple, a lawyer
- Raymond Mhlaba, a protest leader
- Dennis Goldberg, a white engineer and activist
- James Kantor, a sympathetic white lawyer
- Rusty Bernstein, a white architect and activist

Charges were dropped against Kantor early in the trial due to lack of evidence as he had little connection to Mandela's group. Mandela believed they charged Kantor in an attempt to frighten other progressive lawyers. Charges against Bernstein were also dropped.

G.P.-S.6128—1956-7—130,000. **S.**

U.D.J. 315.

Aan

Die Magistraat, distrik _Johannesburg_

Die Vrederegter, wyk_____, distrik_____

Aansoek ingevolge artikel 28 van Wet No. 56 van 1955 om Bevelskrif tot Inhegtenis neming.

Hierby word aansoek gedoen om uitreiking van 'n bevelskrif ot inhegtenis-neming van _NELSON MANDELA_ op 'n beskuldiging van _C/A 2 121·8/1953_

aangesien daar volgens beëdigde verklaring redelike gronde vir verdenking teen hom ~~hoes~~

bestaan dat die beweerde ~~oortreding~~ misdaad begaan is op of omtrent die periode _26.3.61_ _9.5.61._ in die distrik _JOHANNESBURG_

(wyk_____), of dat dit bekend is of vermoed word dat genoemde _BESK._ op die oomblik in die distrik _JOHANNES_

(wyk_____) is.

Staatsaanklaer

Mandela's original arrest warrant, issued by the South African government on May 18, 1961 cause. Freedom was vitally important to them and to all black South Africans.

The ideas Mandela represented frightened a number of white South Africans. They feared losing their status as the higher social class if black South Africans were granted equality. They wanted to stop Mandela.

FIGHTING FOR FREEDOM

To continue the work of freedom fighting, Mandela made many sacrifices. He left his family and lived in hiding, moving from place to place, never sure who he could trust. The government and the police tried for several years to capture Mandela, but he always eluded them. Mandela had many friends, some black and some white, who hid him and helped him do his work.

Mandela's arrest in 1962 was a victory for the leaders of apartheid and a setback for the freedom movement. His capture made headlines around the world. More

Anglo Africans and Afrikaners

White South Africans are divided by language into two groups: English-speaking whites and Afrikaans-speaking whites. Also known as Anglo Africans, those whites who speak English are mostly of British descent. Afrikaans-speaking whites are known as Afrikaners. Afrikaans is a language that developed from the Dutch in the 1800s.

Apartheid was established by the dominant Afrikaners group, with varying support levels from English speakers.

This sign at a beach is one example of apartheid in South Africa. Under apartheid, whites and nonwhites were separated in public places.

and more people became aware of Mandela's work. Black South Africans rallied around him in the effort to free him from prison. Even from behind bars, awaiting trial, Mandela gave leadership to the freedom movement. He became an internationally known figure, representing the fight against injustice in South Africa.

Support for Mandela came from South Africa and beyond. Countries worldwide understood his work. The United States was engaged in its own civil rights movement at the time. Many other

African nations had fought liberation struggles to end oppressive European colonial rule. During Mandela's trial, the United Nations placed sanctions on South Africa for the first time. Economic sanctions against South Africa meant that member nations were not allowed to buy from or sell goods to that country. Many world leaders strongly disapproved of apartheid and the way blacks were being treated in South Africa.

Mandela was devastated when he was arrested. He wanted to continue his work, but he knew the struggle for freedom would continue without him. Mandela was so committed to the movement that he was willing to stand by his actions in court. Mandela did this knowing that he could be sentenced to death if the judge found him guilty. He refused to deny what he had done. He believed he was right.

Mandela accepted the possibility of the death penalty regretfully but bravely. The trial offered the opportunity for him to speak and defend the goals of the freedom movement. This was more important to him than trying to avoid going to jail. Mandela and the other accused men entered the courtroom with plans to admit their actions but blame apartheid for forcing them to the extreme.

Caged in Court

When the Rivonia Trial defendants were led into court on the second day of the trial, they were forced to sit in a huge wire cage. From inside it, they could not talk to their lawyers, who were told to stay outside. None of the lawyers had ever seen such a thing done in a courtroom.

One of Mandela's friends jokingly put up a sign on the cage that read, "Dangerous. Please Do Not Feed." There was some truth in the joke because the idea of caging the men like animals symbolized the government's fear of black activists. The lawyers argued that the cage was humiliating, and they refused to continue with the case until it was removed from the courtroom. The cage was removed the next day.

MANDELA'S SPEECH

The defense opened its case with a statement from the dock by Mandela. He had carefully planned what he was going to say. His words were selected to convey every thought about justice and equality that the freedom movement represented. The prosecutor was furious that Mandela's testimony came in the form of a speech rather than as witness testimony. If Mandela had testified, he would have been required to answer difficult questions posed by the prosecutor. He would not have been able to speak freely. His speech went unchallenged. Mandela spoke for four hours about the freedom movement, the things he had done to further it, and the ideas that drove him to seek change. His eloquence captivated everyone in the room. Mandela concluded his remarks by saying,

During my lifetime I have dedicated myself to this struggle of the African people. I have fought against white domination, and I have fought against black domination. I have cherished the ideal of a democratic and free society in which all persons live together in harmony and with equal opportunities. It is an ideal which I hope to live for and to achieve. But if needs be, it is an ideal for which I am prepared to die.[3]

Total silence filled the room. Mandela finished speaking and sat down. For a long moment, no one moved or spoke. Finally, Quartus de Wet, the judge presiding over the case, continued the trial proceedings, but even he had been affected by Mandela's words.

The Verdict

The trial lasted several months. On Thursday, June 11, 1964, Justice de Wet recalled the court to deliver the verdict. He found Mandela and seven of the ten men guilty. De Wet told them he would assign sentences the next day.

Sitting in their jail cells below the courtroom that night, Mandela and his friends made a difficult decision. The guilty verdict meant the death penalty would probably be given to Mandela, if not the

First Treason Trial

The Rivonia Trial was not the first time Mandela was tried for treason, or trying to overthrow the government. He was arrested for treason in December 1956. His trial lasted more than four years. He was found not guilty.

others. Their lawyers urged the men to consider filing an appeal with a higher court in an attempt to reverse the verdict. Mandela knew the guilty verdict would anger his supporters and spur them into action. It was important to Mandela that supporters be allowed to fight for him. The appeal process would undermine the finality of the verdict against him. The people would have to wait perhaps another year or more to fight the sentence. He did not want them to wait. The time had come for them to fight. The men agreed not to appeal the sentence, no matter what it was. They decided to accept the punishment, knowing that a huge public outcry would occur. The people of South Africa would fight harder to change the system in order to save Mandela from death.

On Friday, June 12, 1964, the accused men returned to the courtroom. De Wet was obviously nervous. His quiet voice trembled occasionally as he spoke the words that would define the rest of Nelson Mandela's life and career and help shape the future of South Africa.

Crowds cheer as a police van brings Nelson Mandela to his first treason trial in Johannesburg on December 31, 1956.

Nelson Mandela was born in the Transkei region in southern South Africa.

CHILDHOOD

Nelson Mandela was born on July 18, 1918, in the tiny village of Mvezo, South Africa. Mvezo is located in the Transkei, a province, or region, in the southern part of the country. His parents named him *Rolihlahla*, which means "troublemaker" in the Xhosa language. He would not be given the name Nelson until he entered school.

Rolihlahla's father, Gadla Henry Mphakanyiswa, was chief of Mvezo. His family history and lineage made him an important man in the community and an advisor to the king of the Thembu people. As the son of a chief, young Rolihlahla would be raised and trained to be an advisor and chief one day. As chief, Gadla had four wives, which was accepted and expected by his culture. Rolihlahla's mother was Gadla's third wife, Nosekeni Fanny. She had her own house and farm, where she lived with her children. Gadla visited often. Rolihlahla was Nosekeni's first child, and he had three younger sisters: Baliwe, Notancu, and Makhutswana.

The status of his father should have given Rolihlahla a comfortable and carefree childhood. However,

The Thembu Tribe

Mandela is a member of the Thembu tribe. The tribe traces its ancestry back 20 generations to King Zwide. The Thembu people traditionally lived in the foothills of the Drakensberg Mountains, but they later moved toward the coast.

The Thembu are one of many smaller ethnic divisions that live in the region, including the Zulu and the Swazi. These divisions have been very important to Africans for centuries. However, once the Dutch and other Europeans claimed power in the region, African people of all ethnic groups were classified as "black" or "coloured." These classifications were distinct from the classification of "white" and served as the basis for apartheid. Despite the fact that the powers of the chiefs changed under white European rule, the ethnic and tribal ancestry and affiliations remain important to Africans today.

Gadla lost his fortune and the title of chief in a dispute with a local magistrate. The magistrate had been put in power by a government that did not respect the Thembu tradition of chiefly authority. Gadla tried to fight the magistrate's new and unfair power but failed.

As a result of Gadla's loss, Rolihlahla's mother had to leave the farm at Mvezo. She moved her children to a new village, Qunu, where they lived a poorer, but happy, existence.

GROWING UP IN QUNU

Rolihlahla's childhood home consisted of three *rondavels*, round huts made with mud walls, grass roofs, and packed dirt floors—a nice home because of his father's status. One hut was for sleeping, one was for cooking, and one was a storage space. His family grew all of their own food: corn, beans, pumpkins, and sorghum. Meals were prepared over an open fire. As young as five

The Chief's Four Wives

According to one Thembu ancient custom, chiefs had four wives. The first wife was called the Great Wife, and the chief would choose his heir from her sons. The chief would also have a Right Hand Wife, a Left Hand Wife, and an Iqadi, or support housewife. Each woman had her own *kraal*, or small farm. Mandela was the grandson of a chief and his Left Hand Wife, which meant he had royal blood. His mother was the Right Hand Wife of his father, who was the chief of Mvezo.

*Xhosa rondavels in the Transkei, South Africa, similar to the home
Nelson Mandela lived in as a child*

years old, Rolihlahla herded sheep and calves, fished, and gathered fruit and roots for food.

When he was not helping with the farmwork, Rolihlahla ran free through the grassy countryside, playing with other boys. At night, his mother told ancient Xhosa tales passed down from other generations. These stories had morals that helped shape young Rolihlahla's identity and world view.

No one in Rolihlahla's family had ever attended school. Education was an informal process in his village. Children learned by watching and listening to adults, absorbing all they needed to know to live successfully in the village. Few of Rolihlahla's neighbors could read or write. A Western-educated friend of Rolihlahla's parents commented that the boy was quite clever. Soon after, Gadla decided to send seven-year-old Rolihlahla to school. Rolihlahla's first teacher, Miss Mdigane, gave him his English name: Nelson.

Mandela's First Suit

As a young boy growing up, Nelson wore a draped blanket as clothing just like the rest of the boys in his village. On Nelson's first day of school, his father took a pair of his own pants and cut the legs to the right length for his son. He took a string and tied the large waist to fit. Nelson later wrote, "I must have been a comical sight, but I have never owned a suit I was prouder to wear than my father's cut-off pants."[1]

LEAVING HOME

Two years later, Nelson's father died. The event changed Nelson's life forever. His mother sent him away to a town called Mqhekezweni to live with his uncle, Chief Jongintaba Dalindyebo, who was the acting regent of the Thembu people. The regent was very powerful, similar to a king or a political leader.

The regent and his wife took Nelson into the family as if he had been their own son. The regent's son, Justice, was about the same age as Nelson. The boys became fast friends, considering each other as brothers, not cousins. They played together, went to school together, schemed together, and got into many scrapes together.

Living in the regent's house, Nelson learned a lot about leadership. He observed the meetings between the regent and his advisors, and the local people who complained, criticized, made requests, and presented arguments. Nelson did not know at the time that this knowledge would help him when he was much older.

Becoming a Man

When Nelson was 16, he and Justice prepared for a traditional Thembu manhood ceremony that is comparable to a bar mitzvah for a Jewish boy. A group of boys of about the same age would gather with community elders for several weeks in special huts that were separated from the town. During this time, the boys would prepare and study for the ceremony.

During the ceremony, the boys received new names to signify their passage into manhood. Nelson received the ceremonial name *Dalibunga*. After the ceremony, the boys were acknowledged as men. They now had the rights and responsibilities of men, such as being eligible to own property and marry. Nelson received a few cows and sheep as a gift. He was proud to have such belongings.

The regent sent Nelson to Clarkbury Boarding Institute, a Thembu secondary school and college. Nelson worked hard. In two years, he earned his junior certificate. In 1937, Nelson transferred to Healdtown, a Wesleyan College in Fort Beaufort. Justice was already a student there. Nelson continued to excel. He earned the respect of his teachers and fellow students. Three years later, he transferred to the University College of Fort Hare. For a black South African at the time, attending Fort Hare was similar to attending a prestigious university such as Yale or Oxford.

At Fort Hare, Nelson was encouraged to study law, but he aspired to be a civil servant, such as an interpreter or a clerk, which was the highest position a black man could hold in South Africa. If he completed three years at Fort Hare, Nelson would earn a bachelor of arts degree. This would give him as many options as a black South African could have. Nelson believed his academic success would help his family members regain their wealth and status, and he looked forward to finishing his studies.

After two years at Fort Hare, Nelson was nominated to the Student Representative Council. He was excited about the prospect of leading and agreed to run. However, the students decided to boycott the student council elections in protest of one of the school's policies. The principal held the election anyway. A few students voted despite the boycott. Nelson was elected. He had participated in the boycott, however, and did not feel that he could accept the vote since most students had not voted. He immediately resigned with the students' support.

The principal threatened to expel Nelson if he did not take his elected position. It was a difficult decision for Nelson to make. School was important, but so was honoring his principles and standing up for

A Model Teacher

One of Nelson's teachers at Clarkbury was Gertrude Ntlabathi, the first African woman to earn a bachelor of arts degree.

his beliefs. Nelson told the principal that he could not change his decision. He left the school one year short of earning his degree. It was the first of many times that Nelson would make a sacrifice in order to uphold his principles. ⌐

South African Geography

For most of Nelson Mandela's life, South Africa was divided into four provinces. From 1910 to 1994, these sections were:

- The Transvaal—the northeast portion of the country. Johannesburg, Soweto, and Pretoria are in the Transvaal.
- The Natal—the western coast of the country. Durban is located in the Natal.
- The Orange Free State—the center of the country.
- Cape Province—the entire south and west of the country. The Transkei, where Nelson grew up, is located in the easternmost part of the province. Cape Town sits at the southwest corner. Robben Island is just off Cape Town's coast.

In 1994, the provinces were reorganized and renamed:

- The Transvaal is now four provinces: Northern, Gauteng, Mpumalanga, and the eastern half of North-West.
- The Natal, except for part of Transkei, is now KwaZulu-Natal.
- The Orange Free State is now Free State.
- Cape Province is now four provinces: Western Cape, Northern Cape, Eastern Cape, and the western half of North-West provinces.

Two smaller countries are also located within the borders of South Africa: Lesotho and Swaziland.

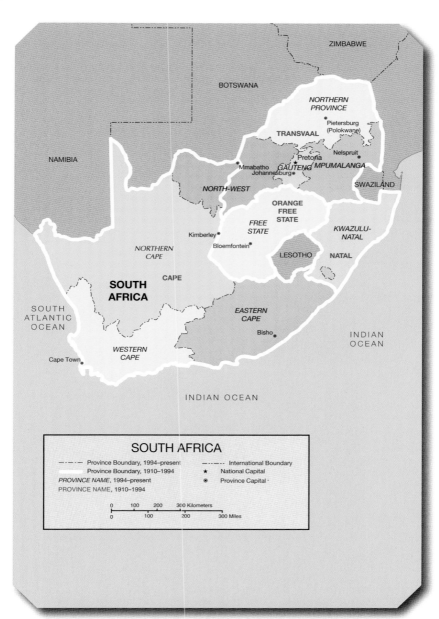

From 1910 to 1994, South Africa was divided into four provinces. Following reorganization, the country now has seven provinces. This map shows the divisions before and after the 1994 reorganization.

Johannesburg, South Africa, in 1938

YOUNG ADULTHOOD

 elson returned to Mqhekezweni uneasy
and frustrated over leaving Fort Hare.
He confessed to the regent what had happened. The
regent refused to accept Nelson's resignation. He
angrily ordered Nelson to return to school in the

fall and join the student council as the principal had insisted. Respect for the regent prevented Nelson from arguing, but he had no intention of returning to the school.

Soon after, the regent decided that both Nelson and Justice needed to marry as soon as possible. He selected wives for each of them. The regent unknowingly assigned Nelson a young woman who loved Justice. Nelson tried to get the regent's wife to stop the wedding preparations, but the regent's decision was final.

Running Away

Refusing to enter married life unwillingly, Nelson and Justice came up with an escape plan. When the regent left Mqhekezweni on a business trip, the boys packed their suitcases and headed for the train station to buy tickets to Johannesburg. At the time, travel was risky for blacks in South Africa because apartheid limited where they could go. Rather than traveling freely, blacks had to carry passes and travel permission slips. It was especially risky for Nelson and Justice to travel, because they did not have the proper traveling papers. Nevertheless, they headed for Johannesburg.

Pass Laws

South Africa's pass laws were used to control the movement of nonwhites. When not in their homelands, every black South African over the age of 15 had to carry a pass book to travel in the country. In addition to requiring a pass book, the laws outlined when a person could travel as well as where and for how long they could travel. The pass book was known as a *dompas*, which is Afrikaans for "dumb pass."

The boys were not aware that the regent knew about their scheme. He had instructed the train agent not to sell them tickets. The two young men were stuck. They convinced the man who had driven them to the train station to take them to the next station, where they were certain they would be able to purchase tickets. The next station was more than 50 miles (80 km) away. Nelson and Justice made it to the next station and bought train tickets to Johannesburg. However, they made it only as far as Queenstown by train. Nelson and Justice were nearly arrested by a Queenstown's local magistrate from whom they tried to obtain legal traveling papers. The magistrate contacted the regent, who wanted the boys sent home. The two young men were able to talk their way out of being arrested, as they had not technically broken the law. The train had gone on to Johannesburg without them, so Nelson and Justice spent most of their money hiring a driver to take them to Johannesburg—a full day's drive away. They reached the city late at night. Nelson had never seen such lights, cars, buildings, and people before. He was thrilled.

In the morning, Nelson and Justice sought work at a gold mine at the city's edge. In addition to arranging a wife, the regent had arranged for Justice to have a clerical job at the mine. Nelson was given work as a mine policeman only after Justice convinced the manager that Nelson and Justice were brothers. Nelson was pleased to have a paying job, but it did not last long. After learning that the young men had run away, the mine manager fired them.

It was 1941. Along with Great Britain, South Africa had declared war on Germany in 1939. The war

Johannesburg

Often mistakenly considered South Africa's capital city, Johannesburg is the country's largest and richest city. A miner found traces of gold in Johannesburg in the 1880s, which led to the discovery of a huge ore deposit. The city became the world's gold capital. This created an economic boom for all of South Africa as people from all over the country and world moved to the city.

The lovely landscape quickly changed as shantytowns appeared. The shantytowns remain, located less than one mile (1.6 km) from the mansions owned by rich residents of the city. These differences aside, the city and its suburbs boast a thriving culture.

Today, mining remains one of South Africa's chief industries. The country's major exports include gold, diamonds, and platinum.

brought a lot of industry to Johannesburg, and
the city grew rapidly. There were opportunities for
work, but many people came to the city seeking the
same opportunities. Nelson hoped his education
would help him get a good position. It took some
time. A friend of Nelson's finally took him to see
about a job in a real estate office run by a black
man named Walter Sisulu. Sisulu liked Nelson and
recommended that he go to work as a clerk in a law
firm.

For the next several years, Nelson worked in a law
firm. He stayed with various families in and around
Johannesburg, paying for his room and board.
During that time, Nelson met many different types
of people and learned a great deal about himself and
the world around him. A number of his new friends
were interested and involved in politics, and he
began learning about that, too. Another black clerk
at the law firm, Gaur Radebe, spoke to Nelson often
about the Communist Party and the struggles for
equality going on in the country. Nelson paid some
attention, but he did not join the cause.

In 1942, Nelson and Justice learned that the
regent had died. They returned to the Transkei but
missed the funeral ceremony by one day. Nelson was

disappointed, but he was struck by the experience of returning to a place that was no longer his home. He then understood that "there is nothing like returning to a place that remains unchanged to find the ways in which you yourself have altered."[1] With his father's death, Justice became regent of Mqhekezweni. He did not return to Johannesburg with Nelson.

BACK TO SCHOOL

Nelson continued his studies through correspondence courses. In 1942, he earned his bachelor's degree and returned to Fort Hare for graduation. His work in the law firm made him realize he could help people if he became a lawyer. A year after finishing at Fort Hare, Nelson enrolled at the University of Witwatersrand to work toward a law degree. He met other young activists and politically interested people. He began to understand the culture of

Suppression of Communism Act

Enacted in 1950, the Suppression of Communism Act banned South Africa's Communist Party and communism. The act defined communism in a broad sense that made any party or person opposed to the National Party government in violation of the act. It essentially made all but the most peaceful of protests a crime. Those found guilty of breaking the law could be imprisoned for up to ten years.

oppression that existed in South Africa and wanted to do something about it.

Walter Sisulu, the real estate agent, gradually became Nelson's mentor. Young activists flowed in and out Sisulu's house, constantly talking about politics, action, and the struggle against apartheid. In August 1943, Nelson participated in the Alexandra Bus Boycott when thousands of workers refused to use public buses. It was his first time in a demonstration. From then on, there was no turning back.

Youth League

Nelson became involved with the African National Congress (ANC). This was the main political group for black people in South Africa. The ANC had existed for many years but was gaining strength in the 1940s. Members had recently selected a new ANC president,

Bantu Authorities Act

The Bantu Authorities Act of 1951 created homelands, African reserves where black South Africans were assigned to live. Africans were assigned to a homeland based on government records regarding tribal ancestry. While homelands were called independent states, they were actually the government's way of removing blacks' South African citizenship and the rights that go with being a citizen.

Alfred Xuma, a doctor. For the most part, the ANC was made up of middle-aged people, many of whom were descended from chiefs.

In 1943, Nelson worked with a group of ANC members to form a Youth League designed to inspire ANC leadership and broaden the organization's membership with more progressive young people. The Youth League was officially formed on Easter Sunday 1944. Approximately 100 men gathered at the Bantu Men's Social Center. Many participants traveled a long way to be there. The group wanted to

African National Congress

The African National Congress (ANC) was founded in 1912 by a group of black South Africans. At that time, the Union of South Africa had recently been formed and had brought Afrikaners and English-speaking people together to lead the nation. Blacks and other nonwhite groups were excluded from politics, which limited their power. The ANC was created to give black people a political voice in the country.

Whites soon created laws that gave white people supremacy over black people. The ANC organized protests and demonstrations to stop these laws. ANC leaders were descendents of kings and chiefs and represented the historical legacy of black power in South Africa. The whites were not willing to listen to them. The ANC's protests died down somewhat over the next 30 years. In the 1940s, when Mandela arrived in Johannesburg, the organization began picking up momentum. ANC members knew they needed to start speaking out and organizing black people.

Over the next 50 years, the ANC led black South Africans in a long fight against racism and oppression. It remains one of the strongest and most active political parties in South Africa today.

revitalize African nationalism by fighting for freedom, democracy, and equality between black and white South Africans.

Nelson began spending more time at Sisulu's home, which became a base of operations for the Youth League. He also met Evelyn Mase, a lovely country girl who was studying to be a nurse. Nelson and Evelyn dated a few months and then married.

Nelson and Evelyn moved into a house. He was proud to provide a home for his family. The couple's first son, Madiba Thembekile, "Thembi," was born in 1946. Nelson enjoyed family life, but he also felt compelled to continue his political work. The sacrifice was difficult, but Nelson believed he was contributing to a greater purpose.

Nelson and Evelyn's Children

Nelson Mandela had four children with Evelyn.
- Madiba Thembekile (Thembi), a son, was born in 1946.
- Makaziwe, a daughter, was born in 1947 and died nine months later.
- Makgatho, a son, was born in 1950.
- Makaziwe (Maki), a daughter, was born in 1953 and, following Thembu custom, was named in honor of the daughter who died as a baby.

A South African shows his pass book. During apartheid, all black South Africans were required to have a pass book in order to travel legally.

Nelson Mandela at the law office he opened in Johannesburg with Oliver Tambo

FREEDOM FIGHTER

he ANC faced its biggest challenge in 1948 when the National Party came to power in South Africa. The National Party was a political group that had openly sided with Germany during World War II despite South Africa's alliance with Great Britain. The National Party's campaign platform introduced apartheid, a system that would formalize and enforce all the laws and practices that kept blacks subordinate to whites in South Africa. Blacks were not allowed to vote in elections, but they were still shocked that the National Party's radically hateful platform had won over the nation.

The National Party enacted its platform immediately, much to the distress of nonwhite South Africans. The government passed a series of laws over the years that made apartheid a frightening reality. Suddenly, every citizen was classified by race: white, Indian, coloured, or black. Unscientific classifications were made based on physical traits or features, such as the shape of a person's head and the color of their skin. A person's race classification dictated where they could live, who they could marry, what jobs they could have, and whether they could

Population Registration Act

Enacted in 1950, the Population Registration Act required every South African to be classified by race into one of four categories. Blacks comprise numerous ethnic groups. The dominant groups are the Xhosa and the Zulu. Whites are English speakers of mostly British descent or Afrikaners. Coloureds have a mixed-race ancestry. Indians are those people from the Indian subcontinent. They are also called Asians in other parts of Africa.

Race was determined by physical features such as skin color and hair type. Once classified, every South African received documentation that clearly indicated his or her race. Reclassification occurred annually.

vote. The National Party was determined to limit the power of nonwhites politically, economically, and socially through apartheid.

Mobilizing Support

In response to the National Party's actions, the ANC mobilized support among blacks. They began to change their tactics. The ANC had always followed the law, but now they began to engage in passive resistance such as boycotts and strikes. Most blacks recognized that more serious measures were needed to fight apartheid. The ANC's president did not want to go along with some of these changes and was soon replaced. Walter Sisulu and several other Youth League leaders were elected to the ANC's National Executive Board. Mandela was voted into the leadership not long after that, becoming copresident. It was a great victory for the Youth League because they had pushed the ANC's main body toward a more revolutionary position.

On June 26, 1950, the "Day of Protest" became the first national political strike organized by the

Freedom Day

Freedom Day is observed on June 26 in South Africa in honor of the Day of Protest held on this date in 1950.

ANC. Black workers stayed home and black businesses did not open. Demonstrations protested apartheid. This date would be honored two years later when, on June 26, 1952, the ANC launched its Campaign for the Defiance of Unjust Laws, or Defiance Campaign. The campaign included violating apartheid laws such as staying out after curfew, using whites-only designated restrooms, and boarding whites-only designated rail cars. Mandela and more than 250 others were arrested for breaking various laws. He spent two days in prison. The Defiance Campaign lasted six months. During that time, the campaign received a lot of media attention. As a result, ANC membership increased from 20,000 to 100,000.

The Defiance Campaign made the government nervous. Government officials began to see what could happen if the nonwhite citizens, who

The Defiance Campaign

During the six months of the Defiance Campaign, more than 8,000 people were arrested and jailed for entering whites-only neighborhoods, ignoring curfews, or using whites-only public facilities. Those arrested spent up to three weeks in jail, and some paid small fines. People nationwide—from all backgrounds, ages, and professions—participated in the protests. Participants knew they would be arrested for their actions, but they were proud to stand up for their beliefs.

The Defiance Campaign gave blacks more confidence in their ability to challenge apartheid. It also made the government recognize that blacks had the power to upset the system. Government officials became wary of the ANC's activities. The government began increasing the laws and restrictions placed on blacks and other nonwhite people. It was only the beginning of the fight between black South Africans and the National Party's apartheid government.

made up the majority of the population, did not agree with the government's policies. In addition, the different racial groups—black, coloured, Indian, and even some whites—had united in strict opposition to the goals of apartheid. The National Party government responded by creating new laws to suppress activists.

First came banning in 1952. A ban was a legal order from the government that not only forced individuals to resign from certain organizations such as the ANC but also restricted them from attending meetings. People could be jailed for violating a ban. Many ANC members were banned, including Mandela, who had been elected national president of the Youth League in 1951.

Mandela and others knew that the government would not stop at banning only individuals. The entire Communist Party was banned, making it an illegal organization. ANC was most likely next. Mandela and other banned ANC leaders created a plan for what to do when the organization became illegal. They had no intention of stopping their work if the ANC was banned, which it soon was.

Mandela continued studying law and took the qualifying exams to become a lawyer in 1951. In

August 1952, he opened a law office in Johannesburg with Oliver Tambo, another black attorney and ANC member.

A troubling result of apartheid occurred when the government began declaring certain living areas open only to whites. In many cases, blacks or Indians were forced to evacuate their homes and move to newly designated areas for their race groups.

The evacuation orders created chaos in several communities. Some people tried to protest the moves. Dozens of people died and hundreds were injured in the demonstrations as the police tried to suppress the protests. The government began putting measures in place to prevent other demonstrations. Still, Mandela continued to fight apartheid. In the early 1950s, he led the resistance to the government's forced evacuation of the Western Areas and its

Ban on Meetings

The bans that the government placed on Mandela prevented him from attending any meetings, political or otherwise. He was not allowed to talk with more than one person at a time. Mandela missed his son's birthday party because it was illegal for him to be around that many people. Banning was a way to limit a person's ability to live without placing him or her in jail.

Group Areas Act

The Group Areas Act restricted people of each racial group to living in certain areas. The National Party government wanted to remove blacks, coloureds, and Indians from certain neighborhoods to make those areas open to only whites. Sophiatown, a historically black settlement of more than 50,000 people in Johannesburg, was one of these areas. The government scheduled an evacuation of Sophiatown for February 9, 1955. For months, the ANC held protest rallies and fought what they considered a strong campaign. On February 9, Sophiatown was surrounded by 4,000 police officers and army troops who began trucking residents out of the area.

The ANC was not prepared to physically fight the army, even though its members had tried to intimidate the government by saying they would die before leaving. Mandela came away from the experience believing that nonviolent protests would not work against apartheid in the long term.

introduction of Bantu education, a system of school segregation designed to keep Africans subordinate to whites in South Africa.

During the early 1950s, Mandela focused his attention on the Freedom Charter, a document adopted on June 26, 1955, by the Congress of the People. The charter lists demands that would create equality among the races in South Africa in all areas of life, including government, housing, employment, and education. The Freedom Charter begins with:

> We, the People of South Africa, declare for all our country and the world to know:
>
> that South Africa belongs to all who live in it, black and white, and that no government can justly claim authority unless it is based on the will of all the people;

that our people have been robbed of their birthright to land, liberty and peace by a form of government founded on injustice and inequality;

that our country will never be prosperous or free until all our people live in brotherhood, enjoying equal rights and opportunities;

that only a democratic state, based on the will of all the people, can secure to all their birthright without distinction of colour, race, sex or belief;

And therefore, we, the people of South Africa, black and white together equals, countrymen and brothers adopt this Freedom Charter;

And we pledge ourselves to strive together, sparing neither strength nor courage, until the democratic changes here set out have been won.[1]

The government did not accept the charter, but instead claimed it as communist. Communism had been banned in South Africa in 1950. As a result, Mandela and 155 other Congress of the People and ANC leaders were arrested and charged with high treason. The group was taken to the Fort, a prison in Johannesburg, where they were held for two weeks.

Ironically, despite the poor treatment the prisoners received, it was a great opportunity for them. The group shared a large cell, where they proceeded to hold "the largest and longest unbanned meeting of the Congress Alliance in years."[2]

Mandela met other freedom fighters within the group who he had only heard of before. The men discussed, planned, and shared ideas and sang together for two weeks while awaiting trial. Though prison is designed to break the spirit, the camaraderie between the men kept them feeling good despite being confined.

Bantu Education Act

Passed in 1953 by South Africa's government, the Bantu Education Act forced black schools run by missions and churches to be placed under control of the government by threatening to cut financial support. Without funding, the schools would not be able to provide an education for Africans, so the missions and churches had to give power over the schools to the government.

The act was another way the government separated the races. It did this physically, by providing different schools for the races, and educationally, by offering different qualities of education for the races—white students were given greater educational opportunities than nonwhite students. The idea behind Bantu education was expressed by Native Affairs Minister Dr. Hendrik Verwoerd, who said education "must train and teach people in accordance with their opportunities" and that Africans had no place "in the European community above the level of certain forms of labor."[3] In other words, a lesser quality education for blacks was fine because they were not going to achieve much in life. This was reflected in the black schools' curricula, which educated students for menial jobs.

Protests were held throughout South Africa and around the world in support of the accused. The 156 accused men were taken to court on December 19, 1956, where the magistrate would determine if enough evidence existed to take the case to trial. After four days, the accused were released on bail, though they were still charged with treason and had to await the magistrate's decision regarding a trial. The magistrate's examination of the evidence took nearly a year. Charges against several men were dropped, but not those against Mandela. He and 95 others were ordered to stand trial—a process that would last nearly five years.

Mandela experienced professional and personal challenges during this time. His law practice suffered. Mandela and his partner, Oliver Tambo, lost many of their clients. Mandela also lost his wife. When he returned home on bail, Mandela found that Evelyn had taken the children and moved out. He was heartbroken but not surprised. Their marriage had suffered as a result of his political work. They divorced soon after.

Though Mandela's life was challenging during the time he awaited the treason trial, he experienced joy as well. He met Winnie Nomzamo Madikizela in

Johannesburg. As the first black social worker in that city, she had great achievements of her own. Like Mandela, Madikizela cared deeply about her people and wanted to help improve their lives. Her political involvement mirrored his. Mandela and Madikizela married on June 14, 1958. They lived simply, by necessity. Of their relationship, he later said, "I never promised her gold and diamonds, and I was never able to give her them."[4]

The trial finally ended on March 29, 1961. Mandela and the others were found not guilty. The verdict freed Mandela, but it infuriated the state. Knowing the government was still watching him, he did not return home. Instead, Mandela went "underground," moving from place to place, hiding from the authorities. ⌐

Nelson Mandela leaves the treason trial in Pretoria, South Africa,
in August 1958, after a day of testimony.

Nelson Mandela led the fight against apartheid in South Africa.

UNDERGROUND

*L*iving underground was a major adjustment for Mandela. He had to leave his family and home to live in uncertainty every day. He rarely stayed long in one place. He traveled from house to house attending meetings and sleeping on people's floors. He tried to avoid appearing suspicious to any police officers. He often posed as a chauffeur, which enabled him to drive freely through the city without attracting too much attention. Reporters started calling him the Black Pimpernel, a nickname that compared him to the main character of *The Scarlet Pimpernel*, a French novel about a man who cleverly evades police.

RIVONIA

After several months of moving from place to place, staying with various friends and colleagues, Mandela settled into a more permanent hideout at the Liliesleaf Farm in Rivonia. The farm offered him a perfect long-term cover. He posed as David Motasayami, the gardener for a white family who lived on the farm. The family knew who he really was, but they were supportive

"Living underground [is a big adjustment]. One has to plan every action, however small and seemingly insignificant. Nothing is innocent. Everything is questioned. You cannot be yourself; you must fully inhabit whatever role you have assumed. In some ways, this is not much of an adaptation for a black man in South Africa. Under apartheid, a black man lived a shadowy life between legality and illegality, between openness and concealment. To be a black man in South Africa meant not to trust anything, which was not unlike living underground for one's entire life."[1]

—*Nelson Mandela,*
Long Walk to Freedom

Before he went into hiding, Mandela boxed regularly. Here, he spars with Johannesburg boxing champion Jerry Moloi in 1957.

of the ANC and the antiapartheid movement. The couple who owned the farm put themselves and their small children at risk to protect Mandela. He was grateful. Soon, several other ANC fugitives came to live at the farm. Secret meetings were often held.

Mandela recognized that the situation in South Africa had become dire. Government controls now prevented people from holding meetings, speaking publicly, and demonstrating—the foundations of nonviolent resistance. The limits on their activities did not suppress the movement. Instead, it made the frustrated freedom fighters look for new ways to fight:

> [I]n the end, we had no alternative to armed and violent resistance. Over and over again, we had used all the nonviolent weapons in our arsenal—speeches, deputations, threats, marches, strikes, stay-aways, voluntary imprisonment—all to no avail, for whatever we did was met by an iron hand. A freedom fighter learns the hard way that it is the oppressor who defines the nature of the struggle, and the oppressed is often left no recourse but to use methods that mirror those of the oppressor. At a certain point, one can only fight fire with fire.[2]

Physically Fit

Mandela was physically fit, even though his exercise options were quite limited while he was underground. He had been a talented boxer in his youth and wanted to keep up his strength. Each morning, no matter where he was staying, Mandela got up very early to run and stretch. Since he could not risk jogging out in the open along the streets, he ran in place indoors. The discipline of daily exercise helped him stay in shape mentally as well. It gave him time to think and clear his mind for the day ahead.

Fundamentally, the ANC was a nonviolent organization, and that would not change. Therefore, in 1961, Mandela, Sisulu, and others formed a new, more militant organization. They called the effort *Umkhonto we Sizwe*, which means "The Spear of the Nation."

UMKHONTO WE SIZWE

The men met secretly to plan a militant response to apartheid. They did not like the idea of violence, but they knew they were already at war—one that was started by the National Party government and waged against black

Colonialism and Revolution in Africa

"The sun never sets on the British Empire" was a famous saying in England several centuries ago. It meant that Great Britain had claimed so much land around the world that it was always daytime in some British colony. During the seventeenth and eighteenth centuries, British explorers sailed to distant places and claimed land for Great Britain. Travelers from other European nations did the same.

The European explorers and the governments they represented did not recognize the ownership of land by the people—Africans, Asians, Native Americans—already living there. They believed whites and the European culture were superior. The Europeans did not understand that African cultures had rich history and traditions of their own and operated civilized societies. Instead, the explorers entered and conquered the lands as colonies for their home country.

From the 1940s through the 1970s, revolutions took place throughout Africa. Africans took arms against their colonial rulers. After centuries of oppression, Africans wanted to reclaim the right to rule themselves. African nations slowly won their struggles for independence. The wars tended to be bloody conflicts, powered by guerrilla warfare.

South Africans. The violence of the apartheid state demanded a violent response. The men considered options ranging from sabotage to guerilla warfare. They did not want to start an open revolution. Too many lives could be lost. Instead, they decided on sabotage—something that would send a message and hurt the government but would not harm many people, black or white.

Umkhonto we Sizwe (or MK) set out to attack the infrastructure—the electric power stations, telephone lines, and government offices. The group coordinated the attacks to occur on December 16, a date celebrated by white South Africans as Dingane's Day in honor of the historical defeat of a Zulu leader by the Afrikaners. That day, MK announced of intentions:

> *Umkhonto we Sizwe is a new, independent body formed by Africans. It includes in its*

Sour Milk

Mandela was nearly arrested due to a bottle of milk. He was staying with a white friend in an all-white neighborhood. He occasionally liked to drink sour, thickened milk, called *amasi*, because the Xhosa people believed it was healthy. To curdle the milk, Africans would leave a bottle on a windowsill in the sunshine for a few days. Mandela did this from time to time, even though he was staying in a white neighborhood. Once, when the milk was on the sill, he heard two black workers outside wondering what a bottle of amasi was doing in a white man's window. Mandela decided to find a new hiding place.

ranks South Africans of all races. … The time comes in the life of any nation when there remain only two choices: submit or fight. That time has now come to South Africa. We shall not submit and we have no choice but to hit back by all means within our power in defence of our people, our future and our freedom.[3]

The success of the first MK attacks convinced Mandela that military action was the right choice. The MK leaders were experienced demonstrators and activists, but they were not trained in military tactics. Mandela needed to learn how to start a secret army, so he turned to people who had done it before. He had many examples to follow. South Africa was not the only African country at war within itself. Throughout the continent, Africans fought for freedom, equality, and control. Countries such as Ethiopia, Ghana, Algeria, and Cameroon had long been colonies of European powers such as France, Great Britain, Germany, and the Netherlands. Now, Africans were throwing off European colonial rule.

Mandela traveled around Africa for nearly a year and a half. He visited Egypt, Ethiopia, Morocco, Ghana, Sierra Leone, Algeria, Mali, and Guinea. He

Nelson Mandela, center, arrives in Pretoria, South Africa, during the Rivonia Trial in August 1958.

Nelson Mandela's prison cell on Robben Island

IMPRISONMENT

O nce he was captured on August 5, 1962, Mandela was charged with encouraging African workers to strike and with leaving the country without proper papers. The charges could land Mandela in prison, but they were not as serious as the treason charges brought against him previously. He knew that meant the state did not have the evidence to link him to MK.

Mandela represented himself in the trial, with help from some other lawyers. He used the court as a forum to speak about his political beliefs. Mandela did not dispute the charges against him, though he made it clear that he did not consider these to be criminal acts. At the end of the trial, the magistrate sentenced Mandela to five years in prison with no possibility of parole.

Adjusting to prison life was difficult. Under apartheid, black prisoners were treated with little respect, just as they were outside prison. They received the poorest food, cells, and clothing. Mandela spent time in solitary confinement after protesting the prison conditions. He found the punishment of solitude far more disturbing.

The Rivonia Trial

Mandela had been in prison nine months when friends began trickling into the jail as prisoners. The police had captured the Liliesleaf Farm hideout in Rivonia. In July

Most Wanted

At the time of his arrest, Mandela was number one on the South African government's list of most wanted criminals.

A Show of Pride

On the first day of his trial for leaving the country illegally, Mandela entered the courtroom wearing a traditional leopard-skin *kaross*. This draped cloth was traditional dress for a Xhosa man. Mandela wanted to show that he was an African in a white man's court. The crowds who came to support him were pleased to see him in his kaross, but the judge was not pleased. He wanted Mandela to wear a suit to court. When Mandela returned to his cell that day, one of the guards came and asked to take his "blanket." Mandela refused to give up his kaross, even when the commanding officer attempted to get it from him. Mandela claimed his right to wear what he wanted and threatened to take the case to the Supreme Court if he was refused. He wore the kaross to court every day for the remainder of the trial.

1963, Mandela was pulled from prison and returned to court. His friends Walter Sisulu, Govan Mbeki, Ahmed Kathrada, and others appeared with him. All faced charges of sabotage and conspiracy to overthrow the government. Death sentences were a distinct possibility.

The yearlong trial ended in guilty verdicts for eight of the accused, including Mandela. Their sentences would come the next day. The men spent a long night waiting between the verdict and the sentencing. They decided that, no matter what, they would not appeal the decision to a higher court. On the morning of June 12, 1964, Justice de Wet announced the sentences: life imprisonment.

ROBBEN ISLAND

Mandela and the six other black men sentenced to life in prison were sent to a facility on Robben Island. They were put in a cell block with a group of 20 political prisoners. Each man had his own small, damp cell with thick walls and hard floors. Mandela's cell had a tiny window that overlooked the courtyard. Each prisoner was given a straw mat, a few thin blankets for a bed, and a bucket to use as a toilet. The cell was six feet (2 m) wide—so narrow that Mandela's head and feet reached the opposite walls when he lay on his mat.

During the day, the prisoners were taken outside and given work. They pounded rocks into gravel for several weeks and mined limestone in a quarry for years. It was difficult physical labor. Often, they were forced to work in

Raid at Rivonia

On July 11, 1963, the Liliesleaf Farm at Rivonia was raided. Mandela had stayed in Rivonia for several months before traveling abroad, so he knew several other people who were staying there. On the afternoon of the raid, a van pulled into the farm's driveway. A young guard on duty tried to stop the van, but it was full of police officers and dogs that jumped out and rushed to the house. They happened to arrive during a meeting of MK leaders. The men tried to run, but they could not get away from the armed police and fierce dogs. Walter Sisulu tried to jump out a window to escape, but he was caught.

Rivonia was a central meeting place and information center for MK. This gave the police access to secret documents, writings, maps, and plans that MK had developed. These materials ended up as exhibits in the Rivonia Trial that began a few months later.

Apartheid in Prison

The rules of apartheid also governed prisons. Food and clothing were distributed based on the prisoners' race classification. Blacks received a pair of shorts, a shirt, and a light jacket. Typically, they were given rubber sandals made from car tires. Mandela received real shoes, but no socks. Kathy, as the only Indian in the group, received socks and long pants. Blacks were fed less food, with no bread. Coloureds and Indians received a small wedge of bread with each meal. The prisoners in Mandela's group pooled food and shared bread and bigger portions among them so that everyone ate the same food. This was their small way of fighting the system, even while behind bars.

silence. When they could, the men passed the time by speaking quietly among themselves about politics. They argued and debated, joked, and told stories. Mandela believes he and the others survived because they were able to be together and support each other. To be left alone in solitary confinement was a torture beyond what he could bear for any long period of time.

Perhaps the most difficult aspect of prison life was the limited visitation allowed on Robben Island. Each prisoner was allowed one face-to-face visit with a family member every six months. Each prisoner could write and receive two letters each year, but the letters were censored by the guards. Sometimes, Mandela would receive a censored letter that had everything blacked out except his name at the top. It was a kind of psychological torture not to be in communication with

Aerial view of Robben Island, where Nelson Mandela was imprisoned from 1964 to 1990

family. The longer a man stayed at Robben Island, the more letters and visits he could receive. Still, that did not happen for Mandela for many years.

Outside Robben Island, the freedom movement struggled. So many leaders were in prison or in exile that few were left to guide the fight. Apartheid took root and developed. Police and government tactics improved at suppressing black South Africans.

Mandela's mother died in the spring of 1968, shortly after making her only visit to Robben Island. The prison denied Mandela's request to attend his

"It is said that no one truly knows a nation until one has been inside its jails. A nation should not be judged by how it treats its highest citizens, but its lowest ones—and South Africa treated its imprisoned African citizens like animals."[1]

—*Nelson Mandela,*
Long Walk to Freedom

mother's funeral. Approximately a year later, Mandela's eldest son, Thembi, died in a car accident. He was not allowed to attend that funeral either. Mandela was heartbroken. It was hard enough to be without his family during their good times. Being separated from them during their difficult times was even worse. By this time, Mandela had been on Robben Island for five years. He still had years in prison ahead of him.

Block "A" of Robben Island Prison, where Nelson Mandela was imprisoned for almost 20 years

Nelson and Winnie walk together after his release from prison on February 11, 1990.

Freedom

The conditions on Robben Island improved somewhat for Mandela as the years passed. He became accustomed to the meager offerings of prison. He began to talk to the wardens, learn about them, and help them understand the reasons behind his work with the ANC and MK. He and his fellow prisoners worked the hard labor they were assigned, but they also exercised their minds. The men developed classes that they taught to the other prisoners on subjects such as economics, politics, and government.

Mandela had been in prison for so long at this point that he was becoming one of the older men on Robben Island. The younger generation of prisoners had a very different political experience of life in South Africa because they had grown up under apartheid. They were very angry and showed it to everyone, even Mandela. He was angry, too, but Mandela showed his anger in a different, more restrained way.

Transfer from Robben Island

In 1982, Mandela and Sisulu were transferred from Robben Island to Pollsmoor, a prison located

"I am fundamentally an optimist. Whether that comes from nature or nurture, I cannot say. Part of being optimistic is keeping one's head pointed toward the sun, one's feet moving forward. There were many dark moments when my faith in humanity was sorely tested, but I would not and could not give myself up to despair. That way lay defeat and death."[1]

—*Nelson Mandela,*
Long Walk to Freedom

in Pretoria, on South Africa's mainland. Mandela had lived on Robben Island for almost 20 years. Pollsmoor Prison had more relaxed policies about visitation and letter writing. For the first time in more than two decades, Mandela was allowed to visit with Winnie and his children in the same room, with no glass between them. They were able to hold hands and hug after so much time apart.

Mandela and Sisulu also received visitors other than their families. Politicians, lawyers, and friends came to see them. Many people wanted to talk to the men about the tense political situation in South Africa. Pollsmoor prisoners were allowed to read books and newspapers; Mandela kept up with current events.

People all over the world knew about Mandela's imprisonment, and he was encouraged by all the

Nelson and Winnie's Children

Nelson Mandela has two daughters with his second wife, Winnie. Zeni was born in 1959, and Zindzi was born in 1960.

Walter Sisulu, Nelson Mandela's mentor, speaks to reporters in South Africa on October 18, 1989, after being released from prison.

media attention his case received. He began to press the government to release all of the political prisoners. His request met resistance from the government, but it was supported by many citizens. The government realized it needed to listen to Mandela. In 1988, the government moved him to Victor Verster Prison. There, Mandela had his

South African President F.W. de Klerk announces the end of all remaining apartheid laws on February 1, 1991.

own small prison house, and he met privately with politicians on a regular basis.

THE BEGINNING OF APARTHEID'S END

Outside prison, the antiapartheid struggle grew stronger. Black South Africans kept fighting for their freedom and for the end of apartheid. The government fought back hard. MK was strong, powered by young men and women who were willing to give their lives for the movement just as Mandela and his friends had done. More and more violence occurred between white and black South Africans. With time, even the strongest supporters began to realize that apartheid could not last.

In 1989, President P.W. Botha resigned. While Botha and other South African whites supported apartheid, not all whites believed in the system of segregation. A segment of the white community understood the need to end apartheid, including F.W. de Klerk. Though still president, Botha had resigned as leader of the National Party while recovering from a stroke. De Klerk was the National Party's new leader, and the party supported him as a replacement for Botha as president

Murder Plot

In 1969, a new young prison guard supervised Mandela's group on Robben Island. The new guard told Mandela that he had been sent to help him escape. Mandela had heard rumors of an escape plan being worked on from outside the prison. The guard explained the plan little by little. It involved a secret key to escape his cell block, an underwater dive, and a boat escape to the mainland, where he would be flown out of South Africa by friends of the movement. Mandela was skeptical of this bizarre plan and the guard. Sisulu agreed that the guard was not trustworthy. Mandela later learned that the young guard was part of an elaborate plot to kill him once he had escaped from Robben Island.

Walter Sisulu

Born on May 12, 1912, antiapartheid activist Walter Max Ulyate Sisulu was the son of an African woman and a white man. As a youth and young man, Sisulu held a variety of jobs: delivery man, mason, carpenter, miner, domestic, baker, paint mixer, tobacco packer, bank teller, advertising salesman, and real estate agent.

Sisulu and his wife, Albertina, were married in 1944. Mandela was his best man. Sisulu was father to five biological children and four adopted children.

Jailed with Mandela on Robben Island for fighting apartheid, Sisulu completed a bachelor of arts degree in art history and anthropology while imprisoned. He was released from prison in October 1989 and elected deputy president of the ANC the following July.

Walter Sisulu died on May 5, 2003.

of South Africa. Botha no longer had full support of his party, and he refused to end apartheid. In response to the changes in power and the pressure to end apartheid, Botha stepped down as president. This was an important event for South Africa. Whites began to realize that apartheid would end. The idea was difficult for many of them to comprehend.

The National Party elected de Klerk as president. He immediately relaxed some of the restrictions placed on nonwhites, including black South Africans. De Klerk allowed peaceful demonstrations and rolled back some apartheid laws. Mandela grew hopeful that de Klerk could lead South Africa toward equality, but he did not let himself hope for too much. He did not want to be disappointed. Only time would tell what kind of leader de Klerk would be.

Mandela and the rest of the world did not have to wait long to find out. On October 15, 1989, de Klerk's government released Walter Sisulu, Ahmed Kathrada, and several other political prisoners. South Africans were overjoyed.

Mandela remained in prison, but with a new sense of possibility. A few months later, on February 2, 1990, De Klerk lifted the ban on the ANC. It became a legal organization again and could hold meetings openly for the first time in three decades.

A Warm Welcome Home

Enormous crowds greeted Mandela upon his release from prison. He expected to see just a few old friends as he walked through the gates to freedom, but he was greeted by hundreds of people. Journalists used cameras and technology Mandela had never seen. He was frightened by the long fuzzy microphones extended toward him because he thought they were some type of weapon.

Mandela raised his fist and the crowd cheered, *"Amandla! Ngawethu!"* He had not been able to do that for decades. A chauffeured car awaited Nelson and Winnie Mandela for the drive to Cape Town, where Nelson was scheduled to make a speech. He had been working on the speech with ANC leaders for several weeks in anticipation of his eventual release. The chauffeur took the couple on a roundabout drive through the countryside in order to avoid the more crowded main streets. Mandela was thrilled to see the trees and wide open spaces he had so dearly missed while in prison.

When the car arrived in Cape Town, it was immediately surrounded by people. Supporters cheered and shouted with joy, knowing Mandela was free. Finally, the car made it to city hall, where Mandela gave his first public speech in almost three decades.

Mandela's Release from Prison

When Nelson Mandela met with President de Klerk on February 9, 1990, he was expecting a typical meeting. He was not expecting his freedom. De Klerk told Mandela he would be released the next day and flown to Johannesburg to greet the public. Mandela wanted to go home as soon as possible, but he asked to be kept in prison for another week. He also insisted that he walk out the doors of the prison rather than be flown out from behind prison walls. De Klerk was shocked at the bold request, but Mandela had his reasons. He thought that the ANC needed time to prepare for his release. De Klerk told Mandela that the press already had been informed of his release date, so he would have to be let go the next day. However, he allowed Mandela to be released directly from prison. Mandela accepted the compromise. It was time to go home.

De Klerk also presented a plan for bringing democracy to South Africa.

A week later, de Klerk visited Mandela in prison. Mandela believed the meeting would be a political discussion. Instead, de Klerk offered him release papers. On February 10, 1990, hand in hand with Winnie, Nelson Mandela walked through the gates of Victor Verster prison a free man.

In a speech given shortly after his release from prison, Nelson Mandela gives the black power salute to a crowd of 120,000 ANC supporters.

Nelson Mandela, left, and F.W. de Klerk pose with their Nobel Peace Prize medals and diplomas on December 10, 1993. They were honored for their work to end apartheid.

CHANGES FOR
SOUTH AFRICA

The last time Mandela had spoken in public was when he gave his four-hour statement from the dock at the Rivonia Trial. On February 10, 1990, Mandela gave a short speech, his first public remarks in more than 27 years. Crowds of people came to listen to and see him in person.

LIFE AFTER PRISON

That night, Mandela returned to his home in Soweto with Winnie. Crowds followed them and stood on the streets through the night, cheering in celebration. Mandela hardly slept during his first night of freedom.

The next day and for many days after that, Mandela attended meetings and made speeches. It was quite an adjustment for him to be near so many people all the time. Much had changed in South Africa and the world during the 27 years he had been in prison. Television journalists wanted to interview him on camera, which was new to him. He had only been filmed once before—going to jail in the 1960s.

Mandela faced a lot of pressure to be the strong leader the South African people expected he should be. They had spent 27 years believing

Mandela's Many Names

Nelson Mandela has had many names:

- Rolihlahla: the name given to him at birth by his parents.
- Nelson: the English name given to him by Miss Mdigane, his first school teacher.
- Dalibunga: the name given to him by Thembu elders during his manhood ceremony.
- The Black Pimpernel: the nickname given to him by the press while he was underground.
- David Motsamayi: his alias.
- Madiba: his clan name, which he grew to prefer over Nelson in his later years.

in and waiting for him, and they had developed high expectations. Mandela quickly got caught up in the nation's needs and his political responsibilities, which did not leave him much time to spend with his family. He regretted not being able to get to know his children better. They had been young when he went to prison, but now they were all grown, some with children of their own. Mandela's family felt disappointed that he had not really returned to them after prison. Instead, he had become the father of all of South Africa.

Mandela's relationship with Winnie became strained during his first few years out of prison. They had spent nearly all of their married life apart, and they had both changed during those long years. The couple realized that the marriage would no longer work for either of them. Mandela

Black South African Nobel Peace Prize Winners

Mandela was the third black South African to be awarded the Nobel Prize for Peace. Chief Albert Luthuli was awarded the honor in 1960 for his work as secretary-general of the ANC. Archbishop Desmond Tutu was awarded the prize in 1984.

announced their separation at a press conference in April 1992. They divorced in 1995.

South Africa's Political Future

Mandela continued to spend most of his time working. He and de Klerk entered a long series of negotiations to determine South Africa's political future. They formed the Convention for a Democratic South Africa (CODESA) to debate the issues. Both men wanted peace in the country, but they disagreed on how best to achieve it. The decision was not theirs alone to make. Mandela had to work with the ANC, MK, and new black groups that had emerged while he was imprisoned. De Klerk needed the support of his cabinet and other National Party leaders. The CODESA discussions began in 1991.

Finally, the negotiations reached a compromise that resulted in an interim constitution being passed in 1993. Whites would have to share power with the blacks and the other nonwhite racial groups in South Africa. Mandela and de Klerk led the way to

Separating from Winnie

When Nelson Mandela announced his separation from Winnie in April 1993, he said, "I part from my wife with no recriminations [bad feelings toward her]. I embrace her with all the love and affection I have nursed for her inside and outside prison from the moment I first met her. Ladies and gentlemen, I hope you appreciate the pain I have gone through."[1]

People's Forums

During his campaign for president in early 1994, Mandela visited many cities and villages across South Africa. They called these town meetings "People's Forums," and Mandela sometimes attended as many as three or four in a single day. People needed to see him and to hear his ideas. He did not want people to vote for him because he was black or because he was a member of the ANC. He wanted their votes because he would bring changes that would benefit them.

The People's Forums also taught people how to vote. On election day, citizens were to put an X on the ballot next to the party they wanted to vote for, such as the ANC or the National Party. None of the candidates' names would appear on the ballot.

a temporary constitution based on democratic principles. A new election for all South Africans would decide the next president of South Africa.

In 1993, Mandela and de Klerk were selected to receive the Nobel Prize for Peace. The process of the CODESA negotiations had inspired people worldwide to look for peaceful solutions to divisive political issues. The negotiations prevented a civil war in South Africa—a victory for everyone.

Mandela Runs for President

Mandela and de Klerk ran against each other in the planned presidential election. There were several other candidates as well. Citizens were eager for the election. Black South Africans, including Mandela, had never voted before. Mandela campaigned for office by visiting villages and townships all over the country. He made many speeches and participated in a debate with de Klerk.

In the process of getting ready for the election, black South Africans worried that the whites might tamper with the election, and ballots were not delivered to some villages. The voting process took four days. More than 23 million people voted.

On April 27, 1994, Mandela became South Africa's first democratically elected president. He took office two weeks later. He was allowed to pick his first deputy president, much like an American presidential candidate selects a vice-presidential running mate. He chose Thabo Mbeki, the son of friend and fellow prisoner Govan Mbeki. Thabo Mbeki was the president of the ANC. Mandela thought they would work well together even though they did not always agree on everything. He was right. It turned out to be a successful partnership.

De Klerk received the second highest number of votes in the election, automatically becoming the second deputy president. He and Mandela had written this rule into the temporary constitution to ensure that no single party would gain full control of the government. Mandela believed the process for creating a new South African government and developing the new constitution should involve people from all political backgrounds to avoid specialized interests. Apartheid had become legal when power was limited to a single group.

A Long Time Coming

On election day in 1994, people arrived at the polls before dawn. They were enthused about the opportunity to vote. Some people waited in line for five hours or more to cast their ballots. "After nearly 350 years, 350 minutes is nothing," one citizen remarked about the wait.[2] This day had been a long time coming, and Africans were determined to make the most of it.

Mandela voted in Durban. He chose a poll site close to where John Dube, the founder of the ANC, was buried. His choice of the voting site was a symbolic reminder of how many people had died struggling to earn others the right to vote. He wanted to honor those freedom fighters who had not lived to see this momentous day. "It was as though we were a nation reborn," he said.[3]

Despite the seriousness of the day, Mandela managed to keep his humor. As he went to the polling booth to cast a ballot for the first time in his life, a journalist yelled out, "Mr. Mandela, who are you voting for?" Mandela called back, "You know, I have been agonizing over that choice all morning."[4]

SEEKING TRUTH

In 1996, Mandela's government presented a plan for healing the nation from the pain of its apartheid past. He called it the Truth and Reconciliation Commission (TRC). Mandela selected a special panel of judges, led by Archbishop Desmond Tutu, to learn the truth about the many sad and violent incidents that occurred during apartheid. The rules of the TRC were that if people told the TRC the truth about things they had seen and done during apartheid, they would not be punished as long as the crimes had been committed for political reasons. All races were encouraged to participate. Mandela believed promising forgiveness for political crimes was the best way to get people to tell the truth. It was important to him to learn the truth from all sides.

Many people became angry at the idea of the TRC. They believed justice would not be served. For instance, black South Africans hated the fact that if a white police officer admitted killing an ANC member during a protest, the police officer would not be sent to jail. They thought it was unfair because so many Africans had been jailed for lesser crimes during apartheid. Whites, on the other hand, wanted Mandela's promise that all crimes would definitely be forgiven.

Mandela knew people would not confess to crimes if they were not protected. He did not think one side or the other would benefit more from the promise of no punishment. He knew there was no punishment that could make up for the loss of life and freedom that had occurred during apartheid. Mandela went

ahead with the TRC, which interviewed hundreds of people over the next several years.

In 1998, the TRC published the results of the interviews in a five-volume report. Blacks and whites alike were upset by its findings. The TRC accused the National Party government of covering up bombings and the ANC of serious crimes. As promised, most of these crimes went unpunished. But Mandela refused to grant full amnesty for all the crimes committed. Cases were considered individually. Amnesty was given for all political crimes.

While president, Mandela concentrated on uniting the country. He left much of the day-to-day government business to Deputy President Mbeki. Mandela clearly wanted Mbeki to become president when he retired, which he planned to do in 1999 at the end of his term. He would turn 80 that year. After 60 years of politics, he was ready for a rest.

Nelson Mandela casts his ballot in South Africa's first democratic election in 1994.

Nelson Mandela and wife Graça Machel attend a fundraising event in Johannesburg in 2005. Since leaving office in 1999, Mandela has focused his energy on humanitarian causes.

LIFE AFTER POLITICS

On July 18, 1998, Mandela celebrated his eightieth birthday by hosting a party. That same day, he married Graça Machel, the widow of a politician friend from Mozambique. The two had become close friends during the last years of

Mandela's presidency. His party guests were thrilled about the wedding. Mandela would have a loving companion to share his retirement.

RETURNING TO QUNU

On June 14, 1999, Thabo Mbeki was elected president of South Africa. Mandela could retire knowing his beloved country was in capable hands. Mandela returned to Qunu with his new wife and built a house. He planned to spend the rest of his days in quiet communion with his family and enjoying the natural surroundings familiar to him from childhood.

Much had changed in his village in the decades Mandela had been away. He now recognized the extent of poverty and hardship that the people faced. His conscience would not let him ignore the struggles of the people he had dedicated his lifetime to protecting. A few years before he retired from public office, Mandela founded the Nelson Mandela Children's Fund to raise money for children's programs and charities. He

Mandela's Home

Nelson Mandela modeled the floor plan of the home he built for himself in Qunu after the floor plan of the prison house where he lived at Victor Verster. He says it is because he liked the design of the prison house and found it comfortable for living.

continued that work in his retirement. Although he had retired, and despite his efforts to lead a private life, Mandela remained a popular public figure.

An Active Retirement

In his retirement, Mandela tried not to be actively involved in South African politics, but his contribution had not been forgotten. His role has become that of a diplomat and statesman rather than an active office-holding politician. In 2000, the United Nations asked Mandela, who had proven himself as a negotiator, to help mediate peace talks to end the ongoing civil war in the African nation of Burundi. He helped bring the nation to a tentative compromise.

Mandela became increasingly concerned about the rapid spread of HIV/AIDS in Africa and around the world. He lost several family members to HIV/AIDS, including his second son, Makgatho. The spread of HIV is preventable, but people do not always take the

Robben Island Today

Robben Island no longer is used as a prison. It has been declared a World Heritage Site by the United Nations Educational, Scientific, and Cultural Organization. Ahmed Kathrada, one of Mandela's fellow inmates, is the head of a museum on the island. Today, visitors to Robben Island can tour the old prison facility and walk into the cell where Mandela was imprisoned for 20 years.

Children at a home for adults and children with HIV/AIDS eat their lunch.

necessary precautions to avoid catching the virus. Mandela began to speak out about the problem, and he worked to convince government leaders that they could help slow the spread of the virus.

In 2001, at age 83, Mandela was diagnosed with prostate cancer. Because the cancer was discovered in its early stages, doctors were able to treat it. Upon his recovery, Mandela resumed his work to help others.

In 2004, for the second time, Mandela formally announced his retirement from public life. Today, he lives quietly with his wife near his hometown of Qunu in the Transkei. Perhaps Mandela would like to fade into the background and enjoy a quiet retirement. The world simply will not let him.

Beloved and respected as he is, Mandela continues to be called upon to make speeches and to represent South Africa in ceremonial ways, though he is less often approached to participate in formal political conversations. At times, Mandela comments on the political decisions made by world leaders. He cares deeply about the world and its troubles, and

A Man to Honor

As a result of his life and work, which have affected countless people around the world, Nelson Mandela has received numerous honors from organizations and countries worldwide. In 1975, a nuclear particle discovered by a researcher in England was named the Mandela particle. The cities of Rome, Italy, and Olympia, Greece, granted Mandela citizenship in 1983. In 1985, the city of London, England, erected a statue of Mandela, while the city of Rio de Janeiro, Brazil, granted him honorary citizenship. In 1993, *Time* magazine named him Man of the Year. In 2001, Mandela was presented with the International Gandhi Peace Prize. Mandela was awarded the Presidential Medal of Freedom, the United States' highest civilian honor, by President George W. Bush.

Honorary degrees have been conferred upon Mandela by numerous academic institutions, including Cambridge University, Harvard University, Howard University, Oxford University, the University of Pretoria, and the Sorbonne.

Public places such as roads, parks, squares, and buildings have been named for Mandela around the world, including in South Africa, India, the United States, and Europe.

he remains committed to helping children and the poor, and fighting the spread of HIV/AIDS.

A Significant Life

Mandela's life has been significant for many reasons. He has experienced much in his lifetime. As a poor country boy with no education, he became a student at the most prestigious school in his country. As a respected lawyer, he became a freedom fighter. As a former prisoner, he became a president. Few people experience such dramatically different circumstances in their lives.

Mandela's story shows that he was brave in standing up for what he believed in, regardless of the sacrifices he had to make. He became a lawyer in a time when black people were discouraged from using their minds. His family life suffered because of his dedication to the freedom movement. He rose above pressure even when his jailers tried to rob him of all hope.

Mandela's life choices show what one person can accomplish. Of course, Mandela would be the first

The Madiba Legacy Series

In 2005, the Nelson Mandela Foundation launched a comic book series titled the Madiba Legacy Series. More than 500,000 copies of the first issue were distributed to schoolchildren to help them learn about Mandela's life and his impact on South African history. Another 500,000 copies were put in newspapers for the general public.

to insist that he did not achieve his successes alone. Many people supported him along the way and made it possible for him to keep living and working. Perhaps that is what makes Mandela's story even stronger.

In 2005, the National Party officially disbanded because few people agreed with its ideas. Party members knew they would never win another election in South Africa. In just over ten years, the powerful apartheid regime had fully collapsed with no chance of returning. For Mandela to see this happen was a particularly special occurrence. Unlike so many freedom fighters, he lived long enough to see the demise of the group whose cruelty had inspired him to fight for justice.

Nelson Mandela has become more than a man. He is a legacy. First a hero for South Africa, people worldwide now look to his example. His life and work will be remembered long into the future. *Amandla! Ngawethu!* —

Paul Kruger Statue

A statue of white Afrikaner hero Paul Kruger, who fought British imperialism in the 1800s, stands in front of the court where the Rivonia Trial was held. The statue's plaque applies to Nelson Mandela's life and work. It reads, "In confidence we lay our cause before the whole world. Whether we win or whether we die, freedom will rise in Africa like the sun from the morning clouds."[1]

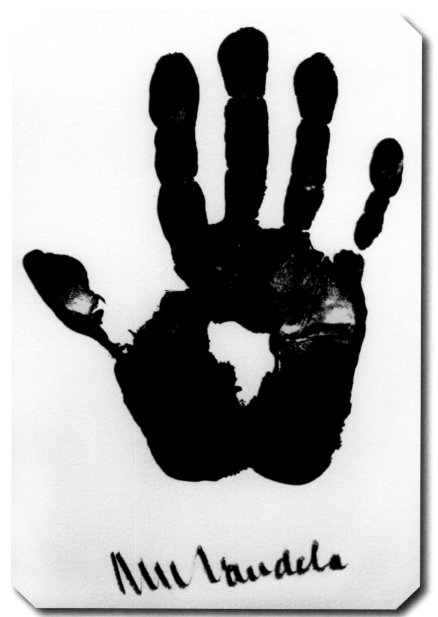

A print of Nelson Mandela's right hand shows what appears to be an outline in the shape of Africa in his palm.

TIMELINE

1918	**1927**	**1930s**
Rolihlahla (Nelson) Mandela is born on July 18.	Nelson's father dies. Nelson stays with the regent, Chief Jongintaba Dalindyebo.	Nelson attends Fort Hare.

1944	**1952**	**1952**
Mandela cofounds the African National Congress (ANC) Youth League on Easter Sunday.	The ANC launches the Defiance Campaign on June 26 with the Day of Protest.	Mandela and Oliver Tambo start Johannesburg's first black law firm in August.

1940

Nelson runs away to Johannesburg.

1943

Mandela enters law school in January.

1943

Mandela marries Evelyn Mase.

1956

Mandela is arrested on December 5 and charged with high treason against the state.

1958

Mandela marries Winnie Nomzamo Madikizela on June 14.

1961

After standing trial since 1956, Mandela is acquitted of all charges. Fearing government hostility, he goes into hiding on March 29.

TIMELINE

1961	1962	1963–1964
Mandela cofounds Umkhonto we Sizwe (MK) on December 16.	Mandela is arrested outside Johannesburg on August 5 and sentenced in October to five years in prison.	The Rivonia Trial is held.

1990	1991	1993
After serving 27 years, Mandela is released from prison February 10.	Convention for a Democratic South Africa (CODESA) talks begin in December.	Mandela is awarded the Nobel Prize for Peace jointly with F.W. de Klerk on December 10.

1964

Mandela is sentenced to life in prison on June 12 and sent to prison on Robben Island.

1982

In April, Mandela and four others are transferred to Pollsmoor Prison in Cape Town.

1988

In December, Mandela is transferred to Victor Verster Prison. He is allowed to meet with politicians privately.

1994

Mandela becomes South Africa's first democratically elected president on April 27. He is inaugurated on May 10.

1998

Mandela marries Graça Machel on July 18, his eightieth birthday.

1999

Mandela retires from public life in June.

Essential Facts

Date of Birth

July 18, 1918

Place of Birth

Mvezo, South Africa

Parents

Gadla Henry Mphakanyiswa and Nosekeni Fanny

Education

Clarkbury Boarding Institute, Healdtown, University College of Fort Hare, University of Witwatersrand

Marriages

Evelyn Mase (1943), Winnie Nomzamo Madikizela (1958), Graça Machel (1999)

Children

With Evelyn: Madiba Thembekile (Thembi), Makaziwe, Makgatho, and Makaziwe (Maki)

With Winnie: Zeni and Zindzi

Residences

Mvezo, Qunu, Johannesburg, Rivonia, Robben Island Prison, Pollsmoor Prison, Victor Verster Prison

MAJOR EVENTS

Mandela was captured and jailed on August 5, 1962. On June 12, 1964, he was sentenced to life in prison but was released on February 10, 1990. On December 10, 1993, he was awarded the Nobel Prize for Peace for his work to end apartheid in South Africa. Mandela became the first democratically elected president of South Africa on April 27, 1994.

SOCIETAL CONTRIBUTION

Mandela spent his life working for racial equality in South Africa. As a member of the African National Congress and Umkhonto we Sizwe, a militant organization he cofounded, Mandela protested apartheid.

CONFLICTS

Mandela and other nonwhites faced great oppression when the National Party came to power in South Africa and introduced apartheid.

QUOTE

"During my lifetime I have dedicated myself to this struggle of the African people. I have fought against white domination, and I have fought against black domination. I have cherished the ideal of a democratic and free society in which all persons live together in harmony and with equal opportunities. It is an ideal which I hope to live for and to achieve. But if needs be, it is an ideal for which I am prepared to die."—*Nelson Mandela*

ADDITIONAL RESOURCES

SELECT BIBLIOGRAPHY

Mandela, Nelson. *Long Walk to Freedom*. New York: Little Brown, 1994.

Meer, Fatima. *Higher than Hope*. New York: Harper & Row, 1988.

Sampson, Anthony. *Mandela: The Authorized Biography*. New York: Knopf, 1999.

Smith, Charlene. *Mandela: In Celebration of a Great Life*. Cape Town, South Africa: Struik, 1999.

FURTHER READING

Denenberg, Barry. *No Easy Walk to Freedom*. New York: Scholastic, 1991.

Downing, David. *Apartheid in South Africa*. Chicago: Heinemann Library, 2004.

Kramer, Ann. *Mandela: The Rebel Who Led His Nation to Freedom*. Washington, DC: National Geographic Society, 2005.

Maharaj, Mac, ed. *Mandela: The Authorized Portrait*. Kansas City, MO: Andrews McMeel, 2006.

Smith, Charlene. *Mandela: In Celebration of a Great Life*. Cape Town, South Africa: Struik, 1999.

regent

> A local leader, similar to the mayor of a city.

Rivonia

> An area in the city of Johannesburg.

sabotage

> An act that intends to harm or destroy something that is useful to someone else.

Truth and Reconciliation Commission (TRC)

> A special court created by Nelson Mandela to interview people about the political crimes and events that occurred during apartheid.

Umkhonto we Sizwe

> The Zulu phrase for "the spear of the nation," this was the name of a South African organization that fought apartheid using sabotage and revolution.

underground

> The act of leaving home to live in hiding from police and the government.

verdict

> The judge's or jury's decision at the end of a trial that declares whether the accused person is innocent or guilty.

Youth League

> A branch of the African National Congress founded in 1944 that brought new, young leaders into the South African freedom movement.

Source Notes

Chapter 1. Turning Point
1. Nelson Mandela. *Long Walk to Freedom*. New York: Little Brown, 1994. 318.

2. Ibid. 355.

3. Ibid. 368.

Chapter 2. Childhood
1. Nelson Mandela. *Long Walk to Freedom*. New York: Little Brown, 1994. 13.

2. Ibid. 95.

Chapter 3. Young Adulthood
1. Nelson Mandela. *Long Walk to Freedom*. New York: Little Brown, 1994. 84.

Chapter 4. Freedom Fighter
1. "The Freedom Charter." 26 June 1955. African National Congress. 12 Oct. 2007 <http://www.anc.org.za/ancdocs/history/charter.html>

2. Nelson Mandela. *Long Walk to Freedom*. New York: Little Brown, 1994. 201.

3. Ibid. 167.

4. Ibid. 215.

Chapter 5. Underground
1. Nelson Mandela. *Long Walk to Freedom*. New York: Little Brown, 1994. 266-267.

2. Ibid. 166.

3. Ibid. 285.

4. Ibid. 306–307.

Chapter 6. Imprisonment
1. Nelson Mandela. *Long Walk to Freedom*. New York: Little Brown, 1994. 201.

Chapter 7. Freedom
1. Nelson Mandela. *Long Walk to Freedom*. New York: Little Brown, 1994. 391.

Chapter 8. Changes for South Africa
1. Anthony Sampson. *Mandela: The Authorized Biography*. New York: Knopf, 1999. 447.

2. Ibid. 482.

3. Ibid. 483.

4. Nelson Mandela. *Long Walk to Freedom*. New York: Little Brown, 1994. 618.

Chapter 9. Life after Politics
1. Nelson Mandela. *Long Walk to Freedom*. New York: Little Brown, 1994. 351.

INDEX

ABOUT THE AUTHOR

Kekla Magoon has a Master of Fine Arts in Writing for Children and Young Adults from Vermont College. Her work includes many different kinds of writing, but she especially enjoys writing historical fiction and nonfiction. When she is not writing books for children, she works with nonprofit organizations and helps with fundraising for youth programs.

PHOTO CREDITS